I0478162

GAME THEORY, AI, AND FINANCIAL STRATEGY

Redefining the Future of Business

CONSULTORIA IA

Copyright © 2024 CONSULTORIA IA

All rights reserved

The characters and events portrayed in this book are fictitious. Any similarity to real persons, living or dead, is coincidental and not intended by the author.

No part of this book may be reproduced, or stored in a retrieval system, or transmitted in any form or by any means, electronic, mechanical, photocopying, recording, or otherwise, without express written permission of the publisher.

Cover design by: Art Painter
Library of Congress Control Number: 2018675309
Printed in the United States of America

TO OUR FAMILY

CONTENTS

BRIEF REVIEW

In a world where rapid technological advancements and economic volatility shape the business landscape, understanding the intersection of game theory, artificial intelligence, and financial strategy has never been more critical. This book explores how these dynamic fields can empower leaders to make strategic decisions, optimize investments, and mitigate risks. By integrating theoretical insights with real-world applications, readers are guided through frameworks that enhance competitive positioning and foster innovation. From predictive algorithms to decision-making in uncertain markets, this book equips professionals with tools to anticipate changes, adapt strategies, and redefine the future of business success.

WHY READ THIS BOOK

Here's why Game Theory, AI, and Financial Strategy: Redefining the Future of Business is a must-read:

1. Navigate Complex Markets: This book provides practical insights into using game theory and AI to anticipate competitor moves, predict market shifts, and make better financial decisions in today's unpredictable economic environment.

2. Harness AI for Strategy: Discover how artificial intelligence can elevate your strategic planning, enabling you to leverage data for improved risk management, enhanced forecasting, and optimized investments.

3. Blend Theory with Practice: Unlike other technical books, this one translates complex theories into actionable strategies, using case studies and real-world applications relevant to finance and business.

4. Gain a Competitive Edge: By combining game theory with cutting-edge AI tools, you'll develop a deeper understanding of competitive dynamics and strategic planning, equipping you to outperform in your industry.

5. Future-Proof Your Business: As markets evolve, so should your strategies. This book is your guide to staying adaptable and proactive, making it essential for leaders, analysts, and decision-makers looking to thrive in the digital age.

TARGET AUDIENCE

The target audience for Game Theory, AI, and Financial Strategy: Redefining the Future of Business includes:

1. Business Leaders and Executives: CEOs, managers, and executives looking to leverage AI and strategic frameworks to strengthen their organization's market position and make informed financial decisions.

2. Finance Professionals and Analysts: Investment bankers, financial analysts, risk managers, and economic strategists who want to integrate game theory and AI into their analysis and decision-making processes.

3. AI and Data Science Enthusiasts: Data scientists, machine learning engineers, and AI enthusiasts interested in applying their technical skills to real-world business scenarios, especially in finance and strategy.

4. Consultants and Strategic Advisors: Management consultants, strategic advisors, and business development professionals who seek to add value for their clients through innovative, AI-enhanced approaches and competitive analysis.

5. Academics and Students: Professors, researchers, and students of business, finance, and economics who want to deepen their understanding of modern applications of game theory, AI, and strategy.

6. Entrepreneurs and Startups: Founders and business owners who aim to incorporate advanced strategic tools to navigate competition, anticipate market changes, and future-proof their ventures in a tech-driven economy.

This book caters to professionals and learners who want to stay ahead in an increasingly AI-driven and competitive business landscape.

PREFACE

In an era defined by rapid technological innovation and economic turbulence, business leaders face unprecedented challenges and opportunities. With the rise of artificial intelligence (AI), the complexities of global finance, and the intricate dance of competitive strategy, the future of business demands a fresh perspective and new tools. Game Theory, AI, and Financial Strategy: Redefining the Future of Business is born from this need to navigate the convergence of these transformative fields.

This book explores the dynamic intersection of game theory, AI, and financial strategy, bridging the gap between theoretical concepts and practical applications. Game theory, traditionally associated with economics and competitive strategy, provides the foundational logic for making calculated, optimal decisions in uncertain or competitive environments. When combined with the predictive and analytical power of AI, game theory transforms into a powerful toolset for modern businesses. AI's capacity to process vast datasets and uncover patterns allows companies to anticipate trends, assess risks, and optimize investment strategies with unprecedented accuracy.

Throughout these pages, I aim to demystify these complex subjects, making them accessible and actionable for professionals in various fields—be they corporate leaders, finance experts, or tech enthusiasts. We will dive into case studies and scenarios where AI and game theory have transformed industries, reshaped markets, and redefined the meaning of competitive advantage.

As you read, my hope is that this book will not only provide you with insights into the future of business but will also empower you to take proactive steps in shaping that future. In the digital age, strategy and adaptability are crucial. May this book serve as your guide to thriving in this landscape, equipping you to make informed decisions, anticipate shifts, and leverage technology to drive success.

Welcome to the journey of redefining business through the lens of game theory, AI, and financial strategy. Let's begin.

CHAPTER 1: THE FOUNDATIONS OF GAME THEORY IN BUSINESS STRATEGY

I n today's rapidly evolving marketplace, where competition is fierce and opportunities are fleeting, business leaders must make decisions faster and smarter than ever before. Enter game theory—a mathematical framework initially developed to analyze competitive interactions in economics, which has since transformed into an invaluable tool in shaping modern business strategies. By understanding the mechanics of game theory, decision-makers can predict competitors' moves, maximize their own advantage, and foster a new era of innovative, resilient strategies.

Game theory was born in the early 20th century, thanks to pioneering mathematicians like John von Neumann and Oskar Morgenstern. Their groundbreaking work laid the foundations for analyzing competitive situations as a structured "game" with specific rules, players, strategies, and outcomes. At its core, game theory is about strategy and, more importantly, strategic thinking—anticipating the actions and reactions of others to secure the best possible outcome.

In business, the "game" is essentially any competitive environment where decisions must be made under uncertain conditions and often with incomplete information. This ranges from product launches and pricing strategies to mergers and acquisitions. Business leaders, whether they realize it or not, play this game every day. Game theory brings a calculated approach to these decisions, giving leaders the tools to make informed choices, even when facing intense competition or rapidly changing conditions.

Understanding game theory begins with familiarizing yourself with its key principles. These concepts serve as the building blocks for developing effective strategies that not only react to competitors but also anticipate and neutralize their moves.

1. Players, Strategies, and Payoffs

Every game in game theory comprises players, strategies, and payoffs. The players can be companies, investors, or any other entities involved in a business transaction. Strategies are the possible actions each player can take, and payoffs represent the outcomes or benefits each player receives based on the combination of strategies selected by everyone involved.

Consider two competing companies launching a similar product simultaneously. Each firm has two strategies: either launch aggressively with high marketing expenditure or adopt a conservative approach to save costs. The payoffs depend on the competitor's choice—each firm must weigh potential revenue against the expense of going head-to-head. Game theory enables these companies to calculate potential outcomes and craft a strategy that balances risk and reward.

2. Nash Equilibrium: Stability in Competitive Strategy

One of the most critical concepts in game theory is the Nash Equilibrium, named after mathematician John Nash. This equilibrium occurs when all players in a game have selected their optimal strategies, and no player can benefit by changing their strategy unilaterally.

Imagine a scenario where two tech giants are considering setting prices for their new smartphones. At Nash Equilibrium, both companies have settled on price points that maximize their profits given the competitor's pricing decision. Any deviation from this equilibrium by one company could lead to reduced profits if the other company does not follow suit.

In business strategy, Nash Equilibrium provides a way to identify points of strategic stability where competitive forces are balanced, allowing companies to make informed decisions about pricing, product positioning, and resource allocation.

3. Dominant and Mixed Strategies

A dominant strategy is a choice that results in the highest payoff for a player, regardless of the opponent's actions. If one company can always benefit from a particular approach, no matter what its competitors do, it holds a strategic advantage.

Not all games in business have a dominant strategy. In complex competitive landscapes, companies may need to adopt a mixed strategy—one that involves varying actions based on probabilities. For example, in the airline industry, companies use a mix of pricing strategies based on peak and off-peak seasons. This approach can prevent predictability, keeping competitors off-balance and allowing for dynamic adaptation to market changes.

Applying Game Theory in Competitive Dynamics

Game theory equips businesses with tools to model competitive dynamics realistically, helping them anticipate competitors' moves and devise responses. Here are some practical applications:

1. Market Entry and Barriers

Consider a new player looking to enter a market dominated by a few established firms. Game theory can help the new entrant understand the potential reactions of incumbents—

whether they might lower prices, launch aggressive marketing campaigns, or form alliances. The new player can then develop strategies to overcome these barriers, potentially collaborating with suppliers or adopting niche market positioning to avoid head-on competition.

2. Price Wars and Product Positioning

Price wars are a common battlefield in many industries, from consumer goods to tech products. By applying game theory, companies can predict the most likely responses to pricing changes. For instance, if lowering prices would lead to unsustainable losses for both firms, game theory suggests that competitors are likely to maintain a stable price. Alternatively, product differentiation can also serve as a strategy to avoid direct price competition, allowing companies to target different market segments without encroaching on each other's territory.

3. Mergers and Acquisitions

In mergers and acquisitions (M&A), game theory can help companies analyze potential synergies or challenges from competitors. If two companies are vying for the same acquisition target, understanding each other's objectives and possible moves can influence bid strategies, timing, and negotiation tactics. Game theory can also support decision-making by revealing whether forming strategic alliances or merging with smaller players would yield a stronger market position than competing against a larger rival.

Strategic Frameworks Inspired by Game Theory

The strategic frameworks derived from game theory are invaluable for businesses seeking to maximize their advantage in competitive environments. Here are some of the most popular frameworks inspired by game theory:

1. Prisoner's Dilemma in Cooperation and Competition

The Prisoner's Dilemma is a classic scenario illustrating the challenge of cooperation between competitors. In business, it's common for two companies to benefit from cooperation but risk losing out if one party acts selfishly. Consider two firms with similar products that decide to keep advertising spending low to maintain profitability. If one firm reneges and increases its ad budget, it could capture more market share, but at the expense of mutual profitability.

This dilemma can serve as a guiding principle in forming partnerships, strategic alliances, and even industry-wide standards. When businesses understand the potential outcomes of both cooperation and betrayal, they can establish trust mechanisms and contracts that mitigate the risks of non-cooperative behavior.

2. The Stag Hunt: Risk and Reward in Joint Ventures

The Stag Hunt scenario illustrates the risk-reward tradeoff in joint ventures or partnerships. In this scenario, two hunters must decide to hunt a stag together (requiring cooperation for a big reward) or hunt a rabbit individually (for a smaller but guaranteed reward). Translating this into business, the stag represents a high-reward venture—such as co-developing a new technology—while the rabbit represents a safer but lower-return investment.

This game highlights the importance of aligning objectives in joint ventures. Both companies must be committed to the larger goal to reap the benefits; otherwise, they risk settling for a suboptimal outcome. Understanding the Stag Hunt dynamic enables companies to assess potential partners, gauge commitment levels, and mitigate risks through strong contractual agreements.

3. Zero-Sum vs. Positive-Sum Games

Not all business interactions are competitive battles where one company's gain is another's loss—a concept known as zero-sum games. In reality, many business situations are positive-sum games, where cooperation can lead to mutual benefit. For example, by forming a cross-industry alliance, businesses can leverage each other's strengths to access new markets, create innovative products, and share resources.

Recognizing whether a scenario is zero-sum or positive-sum helps companies choose the appropriate strategies and fosters a mindset geared towards win-win outcomes.

Building a Game Theory-Driven Decision-Making Framework

The potential of game theory in business lies in its structured approach to decision-making. With game theory as a foundation, companies can create a robust framework for analyzing competitive dynamics, forecasting outcomes, and making strategic decisions that enhance resilience and flexibility.

1. Identify the Players – Define the key players in your market, including direct competitors, potential entrants, and influential stakeholders.

2. Map Possible Strategies – Outline potential strategies for each player. This could include pricing, market positioning, or new product launches.

3. Estimate Payoffs and Consequences – Evaluate the potential outcomes for each strategy combination. Consider short-term gains and long-term effects on market share, profitability, and reputation.

4. Determine Optimal Strategy Combinations – Using models like Nash Equilibrium, identify strategy combinations that offer stability and maximize benefits for your business under current conditions.

As we stand on the brink of an era dominated by artificial intelligence and machine learning, game theory is becoming increasingly integral to business strategy. With AI, companies can process vast amounts of data to model competitive scenarios in real-time, enhancing their ability to predict outcomes and adapt strategies dynamically. From finance to tech, and from healthcare to retail, game theory is no longer confined to academia; it's a practical tool for any organization that aims to excel in a complex, interconnected, and highly competitive world.

Game theory has become one of the most pivotal frameworks for analyzing competitive environments in business. By applying game theory's principles—such as Nash Equilibrium, mixed strategies, and optimal decision-making—businesses gain a strategic advantage in navigating competition, pricing strategies, partnerships, and other crucial decisions. However, game theory's full potential comes to life when real-world examples are examined, showing its applicability in shaping global industries and high-stakes business decisions.

Real-World Applications of Game Theory in Business

1. Pricing Wars in the Airline Industry

In the airline industry, one of the most prevalent applications of game theory involves pricing strategies. With numerous competitors in the market, the decision to set a ticket price is not made in isolation. Instead, it depends heavily on the expected reactions from rival airlines. This is a clear example of strategic interdependence, a central tenet of game theory.

Consider the competition between Delta and American Airlines. If Delta reduces ticket prices to capture a larger share of the market, American Airlines might lower their prices in retaliation, resulting in a price war. This could lead to reduced profits for both companies. However, if both airlines keep their prices stable and focus on customer service or loyalty programs instead, they can maintain profitability without triggering a destructive price war.

A well-known case in this industry is the airline fare wars of the 1990s, when major U.S. carriers would often mirror each other's pricing moves within hours. According to an analysis by Harvard Business Review, U.S. airlines lose billions of dollars each year due to aggressive price competition. Game theory helps to predict whether airlines will engage in price cuts or seek alternative strategies, such as offering value-added services, partnerships, or alliances.

The concept of Nash Equilibrium can be observed in this scenario—both airlines are likely to find a pricing point that maximizes their profits given the pricing decisions of the other. If both airlines know that lowering prices will hurt them more than it benefits them, they may reach an equilibrium where neither lowers prices.

2. The Oligopolistic Market of Smartphones

The global smartphone market, dominated by Apple, Samsung, and Huawei, serves as a perfect example of game theory in action. These companies engage in fierce competition, with each trying to anticipate the next move of their rivals in terms of new product features, marketing strategies, and, of course, pricing.

In 2019, for instance, Apple released its iPhone 11 series, while Samsung unveiled the Galaxy Note 10 at nearly the same time. Both companies had to consider the pricing, advertising, and feature positioning of each other's devices. If one company released a more advanced product at a lower price, the other would likely respond with a similar offering to maintain its market share.

Game theory models the possible strategic decisions of each player, anticipating whether they will choose to innovate (e.g., Apple's introduction of Face ID) or to undercut each other on price (e.g., Samsung offering discounts on Galaxy S models). Nash Equilibrium comes into play when both companies realize that introducing a cutting-edge product at a higher price could be the optimal strategy, provided that both keep their price points aligned, which benefits them both more than entering a price war.

This type of decision-making has massive financial implications. In the smartphone industry, global revenues surpassed $520 billion in 2023, with Apple and Samsung commanding over 50% of the market share, according to IDC data. Game theory offers these companies a strategic map for making the most effective decisions within this highly competitive and lucrative market.

3. Collaboration vs. Competition in the Pharmaceutical Industry

The pharmaceutical industry is another area where game theory plays a significant role, particularly in situations involving collaboration versus competition. For instance, two pharmaceutical companies, AstraZeneca and Pfizer, have both developed COVID-19 vaccines. Instead of direct competition, these companies chose to cooperate with one another to increase the global supply of vaccines.

This collaboration, rather than competition, reflects the Stag Hunt game theory model, where the joint reward is far greater than individual efforts. Had AstraZeneca and Pfizer chosen not to cooperate, they might have faced significant market barriers and delays in vaccine production, reducing their respective payoffs. Instead, they opted for shared development and distribution, resulting in greater success for both companies and a significant public health impact.

The total global vaccine market is expected to exceed $60 billion by 2030 according to Grand View Research, showing just how lucrative this industry can be. In such a scenario, game theory provided these companies with a strategic framework to understand that collaboration could lead to a mutually beneficial, positive-sum outcome, which in turn benefits society as a whole.

4. Mergers and Acquisitions: The Case of Disney and 21st Century Fox

Mergers and acquisitions (M&A) are one of the most high-stakes strategic decisions that businesses can make. Game theory provides companies with the tools to model various strategic moves when contemplating a merger or acquisition. A prime example of game theory's relevance in M&A is the 2017 acquisition of 21st Century Fox by The Walt Disney Company.

Disney's decision to acquire Fox was a complex game involving multiple players, including Comcast, who was also interested in acquiring the same assets. In such high-stakes scenarios, companies utilize game theory to assess the payoffs of different bids, the potential reactions of the target company, and the likely moves of competitors.

By applying Nash Equilibrium and other game theory principles, Disney predicted that making an all-cash offer would outpace Comcast's all-stock bid, compelling Fox to agree to Disney's acquisition offer. The deal, worth $71.3 billion, was not just about acquiring assets but also securing a strategic position in the media industry to compete with streaming giants like Netflix and Amazon Prime.

This acquisition illustrates how game theory allows a company to assess the most advantageous strategy in a bidding war, taking into account the possible moves of competitors, the payoff of the acquisition, and the long-term strategic benefits. In this case, Disney emerged victorious, strengthening its content library and expanding its reach in the streaming market, particularly through its Disney+ platform.

Integrating AI and Game Theory for Enhanced Decision-Making

As artificial intelligence (AI) becomes more integral to business operations, its integration with game theory is revolutionizing how companies strategize. AI models can process massive amounts of data and simulate countless scenarios to forecast the outcomes of various decisions. This capability is particularly useful in competitive and market-driven environments where timely, data-driven decisions are crucial.

AI in Real-Time Decision Making

Imagine an e-commerce company like Amazon, which competes with global retailers such as Walmart and Alibaba. By employing AI algorithms powered by game theory principles, Amazon can monitor competitor prices, consumer behavior, and market trends in real time, adjusting its pricing strategy to maximize profit without triggering a price war.

For instance, Amazon uses dynamic pricing algorithms that adjust prices every 10 minutes, based on competition and demand. Game theory allows Amazon's AI systems to predict whether a competitor will react to a price drop and how much benefit Amazon stands to gain by lowering or raising prices. This type of mixed strategy creates a competitive advantage by outmaneuvering rivals while ensuring profit margins remain intact.

AI and Predictive Analytics in Financial Markets

Game theory, combined with AI, is also transforming the way businesses approach financial risk management. In stock markets, for example, algorithmic trading uses AI models to forecast potential moves by competitors based on real-time market data. By simulating thousands of potential scenarios, AI models can predict price movements and suggest optimal trading strategies.

In the forex market, where trillions of dollars are exchanged daily, AI-driven game theory models help traders identify patterns, evaluate potential risks, and simulate competitor moves. For example, during a volatile market event like Brexit, AI systems modeled the decisions of hedge funds and other market players, providing real-time strategies to capitalize on the event's fallout.

According to Statista, the total global value of the foreign exchange market was over $6.6 trillion per day in 2023, with game theory and AI tools playing an increasingly important role in influencing decisions made by financial institutions and investors.

Game theory provides a powerful framework for navigating the complexities of business strategy in the digital age. By understanding the underlying principles of competition, cooperation, and decision-making, business leaders can craft strategies that maximize value, anticipate competitor moves, and thrive in dynamic markets. Whether it's through strategic pricing in the airline industry, cooperation in pharmaceuticals, or optimizing M&A decisions, game theory proves to be indispensable in shaping business success.

In the coming chapters, we will explore how artificial intelligence amplifies these game theory principles, bringing predictive power and strategic foresight to the decision-making process. As we advance into the future, the convergence of game theory and AI will not only redefine the way businesses compete but also offer new opportunities for collaboration and growth in an increasingly interconnected world.

CHAPTER 2: LEVERAGING AI FOR PREDICTIVE FINANCIAL INSIGHTS

The fusion of artificial intelligence (AI) and finance is reshaping the way businesses approach forecasting, risk assessment, and investment strategies. What once required vast teams of analysts and countless hours of manual work can now be achieved with unmatched speed and precision using AI-powered algorithms. In this chapter, we'll delve into how AI is transforming predictive financial insights and revolutionizing the way businesses navigate complex financial landscapes. We'll explore the specific tools, techniques, and methodologies that are setting new standards in financial forecasting and investment strategy.

Understanding the Role of AI in Financial Forecasting

Financial forecasting involves predicting future financial outcomes based on historical data and market trends. Traditionally, financial analysts relied heavily on historical records, statistical models, and complex spreadsheets to generate forecasts. However, these methods often fell short in volatile markets, where trends can change in a heartbeat.

AI, particularly machine learning (ML) and deep learning, has introduced a game-changing approach to forecasting. Through algorithms capable of analyzing massive datasets in real-time, AI identifies patterns and relationships that are otherwise invisible to the human eye. These insights allow businesses to adjust strategies in real-time, mitigating risks and maximizing returns.

Machine learning models have brought financial forecasting to a new level of sophistication. For instance, supervised learning models can be trained on historical financial data to predict future outcomes with increased accuracy. Unsupervised learning, meanwhile, can uncover hidden correlations in the data, allowing businesses to gain valuable insights into emerging trends and changing consumer behaviors.

Case Study: Predicting Stock Market Movements with AI

A prominent example of AI-driven forecasting in action is in the stock market. By analyzing massive amounts of historical data, including price movements, trading volumes, and even social media sentiment, AI models can predict price trends with impressive accuracy. Hedge funds and institutional investors are increasingly turning to AI models to generate "alpha" — the excess returns over market benchmarks.

Companies like Renaissance Technologies and Two Sigma have pioneered the use of AI in investment strategy. They employ machine learning algorithms that detect complex patterns in financial data, leading to predictions that would be impossible for human analysts to uncover manually. These firms spend millions annually on data infrastructure and algorithm refinement, emphasizing the value and potential of AI in delivering an edge in highly competitive financial markets.

AI-Powered Risk Assessment: Reducing Uncertainty in Finance

Risk assessment is a critical component of financial strategy, encompassing credit risk, market risk, operational risk, and more. AI's ability to analyze data at a granular level allows companies to assess these risks with greater precision and in real-time. Machine learning models, for example, can evaluate credit risk by examining a customer's historical spending habits, social media activity, and other behavioral data points — not just their credit score. This holistic approach provides a far more accurate view of an individual's creditworthiness.

Credit Risk Assessment with AI

Credit risk is one of the areas where AI has made remarkable strides. Traditionally, banks and financial institutions relied on static models, such as credit scoring systems, to determine the likelihood of default. However, these models often fail to account for variables that indicate real-world risk dynamics.

AI-based credit risk models, in contrast, can incorporate a wide array of data sources, from payment history to social behavior. This allows lenders to assess risk more comprehensively, enabling them to offer loans at more competitive rates while minimizing the likelihood of default. Lenders can analyze not only quantitative data, like income and expenses, but also qualitative data, like social media behavior and even GPS data, which can offer insights into spending habits and lifestyle stability.

Market Risk Management with Machine Learning

Market risk is another area where AI-driven insights are proving invaluable. Financial markets are highly volatile, and traditional methods of assessing market risk often fail to respond to sudden, unforeseen changes. AI enables real-time risk management, allowing firms to adjust their strategies instantaneously.

For instance, hedge funds use machine learning algorithms to assess the potential risks of their portfolios under different market conditions. These models can simulate scenarios, such as recessions, geopolitical events, or changes in interest rates, and analyze their potential impacts on the portfolio. By running thousands of simulations, AI models help firms optimize their investments while minimizing exposure to adverse conditions.

Fraud Detection and Prevention

AI is also transforming the field of fraud detection, a critical aspect of risk management in finance. Fraudulent activities can cost companies millions and damage their reputations. AI algorithms can detect anomalies in transaction data, flagging potentially fraudulent activity in real-time. These algorithms are continuously learning from new data, which helps them stay ahead of evolving fraud tactics.

Financial institutions, for instance, use AI to detect unusual transaction patterns that might indicate fraud. If an algorithm detects a series of unusual transactions — such as a large withdrawal from a new location — it can automatically trigger a security alert, potentially saving the bank and its customers from significant losses. AI-driven fraud detection not only enhances security but also builds trust among customers, who can feel confident that their finances are being protected.

Optimizing Investment Strategies with AI

Investment strategy is perhaps one of the most exciting applications of AI in finance. By analyzing historical market data, economic indicators, and alternative data sources like social sentiment, AI can generate high-potential investment strategies with reduced human intervention. Hedge funds, asset managers, and retail investors alike are leveraging AI to refine their portfolios and make more informed investment decisions.

Quantitative Trading Models

Quantitative trading, or "quant trading," relies on mathematical models to make investment decisions. These models are now heavily augmented by AI, enabling traders to make split-second decisions based on real-time data. Quant trading algorithms can analyze historical data, news articles, earnings reports, and even weather patterns to predict price movements and execute trades automatically.

One of the biggest advantages of AI in quant trading is its ability to identify arbitrage opportunities — price discrepancies in different markets — which can be exploited for profit. For example, if an AI model detects that a stock is underpriced on one exchange compared to another, it can execute trades to profit from the discrepancy. This requires processing immense amounts of data in milliseconds, something that AI excels at and human traders simply cannot match.

Portfolio Optimization

Portfolio optimization involves selecting a mix of assets that align with an investor's risk tolerance and financial goals. Traditionally, portfolio managers relied on mean-variance optimization (MVO), a statistical technique that seeks to maximize returns for a given level of risk. However, MVO models often fall short because they rely on assumptions about market behavior that do not hold in volatile markets.

AI offers a more dynamic approach to portfolio optimization. By incorporating real-time data and adjusting to changing market conditions, AI-powered models provide a portfolio strategy that can be adjusted in real-time. These models can optimize portfolios not just for traditional risk-return balance but also for specific goals, such as maximizing environmental, social, and governance (ESG) criteria or aligning with thematic trends like renewable energy.

Machine Learning Techniques Driving Predictive Financial Insights

Several machine learning techniques are powering these AI-driven insights in finance. Below are a few of the most impactful methodologies that are transforming financial forecasting and strategy.

1. Regression Analysis

Regression analysis is a statistical technique that identifies relationships between variables. In finance, regression models are commonly used to predict asset prices, interest rates, and other key metrics. Machine learning has advanced regression analysis by enabling it to handle larger, more complex datasets with greater accuracy. For instance, regression models can analyze historical data to forecast stock prices based on factors such as earnings, economic indicators, and social sentiment.

2. Time Series Analysis

Time series analysis is essential in finance, where predicting future prices and trends based on historical data is key. Traditional time series models, like ARIMA, have been used for decades, but they are limited in handling the complexity and volume of modern financial data. Machine learning models, such as recurrent neural networks (RNNs) and long short-term memory (LSTM) networks, excel in processing sequential data, making them ideal for financial forecasting. These models can analyze patterns in historical price data, offering more accurate predictions about future price movements.

3. Natural Language Processing (NLP)

Natural language processing, a branch of AI that deals with human language, has opened up new possibilities for financial forecasting and strategy. By analyzing text data from news articles, earnings calls, and social media, NLP models can gauge public sentiment about a particular stock or market. Sentiment analysis, for instance, has become a popular tool in predicting short-term market movements. A spike in positive sentiment around a company, as detected by NLP algorithms, can lead to increased demand for its stock.

4. Reinforcement Learning

Reinforcement learning is an area of machine learning that teaches algorithms to make decisions by rewarding positive actions and penalizing negative ones. In finance, reinforcement learning can be used to train algorithms that continuously adapt to market conditions. For example, reinforcement learning models can be used to develop trading strategies that adjust to different market environments, maximizing returns over time.

The Future of AI in Predictive Financial Insights

AI's role in finance is expected to grow significantly in the coming years. With advancements in data collection and processing power, AI will continue to offer increasingly sophisticated tools for forecasting, risk management, and investment strategy. Some areas likely to see growth include:

1. Personalized Financial Planning: AI can provide individualized financial insights for retail investors, offering tailored investment strategies based on personal risk tolerance and financial goals.

2. Real-Time Predictive Analytics: As AI systems become more integrated with financial markets, businesses will be able to make real-time predictions and react instantly to market changes.

3. Ethics and Transparency in AI Models: As AI becomes a cornerstone of financial strategy, transparency and accountability in AI-driven decisions will become crucial. Regulators and institutions will need to develop standards to ensure that AI is used ethically and responsibly.

4. Cross-Industry Financial Insights: AI's ability to analyze unstructured data will allow businesses to pull insights from other industries, providing a more comprehensive view of factors impacting financial decisions.

AI has introduced a paradigm shift in finance, allowing businesses to leverage predictive insights that were once unattainable. Through machine learning and data analysis, companies can forecast with unprecedented accuracy, assess risks more comprehensively, and create investment strategies that maximize returns while minimizing exposure. The adoption of AI-driven financial strategies is no longer optional; it's becoming a critical component for success in the modern business landscape.

In the coming years, AI will not only redefine financial strategy but also bring a new level of precision and adaptability to the way we understand and respond to market dynamics. As businesses continue to harness the power of AI, the future of finance promises to be one where strategy is driven not by instinct, but by data-driven, intelligent insights that pave the way for sustainable growth and innovation.

Practical Applications of AI in Financial Forecasting and Investment Strategies

The theoretical capabilities of AI in finance are compelling, but the practical applications are where the true value of these technologies shines. In this chapter, we'll explore how artificial intelligence is applied in real-world financial forecasting, risk assessment, and investment strategy. We'll dive into specific examples and provide numerical and mathematical insights to show exactly how AI is reshaping the finance industry.

1. Predicting Stock Prices with Time Series Analysis

Case Study: Forecasting Stock Prices for Tesla Inc. (TSLA)

Let's consider a case study involving Tesla Inc. (TSLA), a stock known for its volatility. Using AI models like Long Short-Term Memory (LSTM) neural networks, we can forecast short-term price movements by analyzing historical price data. LSTMs are particularly well-suited for time series data due to their ability to retain information over long sequences of time, making them effective at capturing trends and seasonal patterns.

1. Data Preparation: Collect daily closing prices for TSLA over the past three years.

2. Feature Engineering: In addition to the closing price, calculate technical indicators such as the moving average (MA), relative strength index (RSI), and volatility.

3. Building the LSTM Model:

  - Input data consists of the past 60 days of prices and technical indicators.

  - Hidden layers are configured to allow the model to learn complex patterns in the data.

  - Output layer provides a predicted closing price for the next trading day.

4. Training and Validation: The data is split into a training set (80%) and validation set (20%). The model trains for a set number of epochs until it minimizes prediction errors.

5. Evaluation: The model's accuracy can be assessed using metrics like Mean Squared Error (MSE) and Mean Absolute Percentage Error (MAPE).

Example Calculation

Suppose the model's output for a given day forecasts a TSLA closing price of $800, while the actual closing price is $810. The prediction error (MSE) for that day would be calculated as:

$$MSE = \frac{(800 - 810)^2}{1} = 100$$

After running predictions over a month, the average MSE can be calculated to gauge overall model performance. A low MSE implies that the model is highly accurate, while a high MSE suggests further tuning is needed.

Quantifying Model Impact

By accurately predicting TSLA price movements, a quantitative trading strategy might execute buy/sell orders based on forecasted gains, targeting, for instance, a 2% daily return. If this target is consistently met over a year, the cumulative annual return could theoretically exceed 700% (assuming 250 trading days):

$$\text{Annual Return} = (1 + 0.02)^{250} - 1 \approx 7.1$$

While real-world conditions might reduce this idealized return, it illustrates the immense potential AI offers in trading when prediction errors are kept minimal.

2. Credit Risk Assessment Using Logistic Regression

Example: Predicting Loan Default Rates

Credit risk assessment is a core aspect of lending, and AI can improve predictions of borrower defaults with logistic regression — a supervised learning algorithm that predicts binary outcomes (e.g., "default" or "no default").

1. Data Collection: Gather data on borrower characteristics such as income, debt-to-income ratio, employment length, credit score, and existing loans.

2. Feature Selection: Identify features that strongly correlate with loan default likelihood, such as low credit scores or high debt-to-income ratios.

3. Model Training: Use logistic regression to map the relationships between borrower characteristics and the probability of default. The model might produce an equation of the form:

$$P(\text{default}) = \frac{1}{1 + e^{-(\beta_0 + \beta_1 \cdot \text{credit score} + \beta_2 \cdot \text{debt-to-income ratio} + \dots)}}$$

, where beta coefficients represent weights assigned to each predictor variable.

4. **Thresholding**: Set a probability threshold (e.g., 0.5) to determine the likelihood of default. If $P(\text{default}) > 0.5$, the applicant is flagged as high-risk.

Example Calculation

Suppose a borrower has a credit score of 600, a debt-to-income ratio of 0.4, and other characteristics assigned weights in the logistic regression model. Using our logistic regression model, we might calculate:

$$P(\text{default}) = \frac{1}{1 + e^{-(1.5 - 0.02 \cdot 600 + 0.8 \cdot 0.4)}}$$

This equation evaluates to a probability, say 0.75. Since this exceeds our threshold of 0.5, the model would classify this borrower as a high-risk default candidate, potentially requiring further review or a higher interest rate.

Practical Impact

AI-based credit risk models have proven to reduce loan defaults by up to 25% while enabling institutions to offer competitive interest rates to low-risk borrowers. For lenders, reducing default rates directly improves profitability and capital allocation.

3. Portfolio Optimization with Reinforcement Learning

Scenario: Optimizing an Investment Portfolio Using Q-Learning

Reinforcement learning (RL) is a type of machine learning where algorithms make sequential decisions based on a reward-punishment framework. Q-learning, a popular RL algorithm, is particularly suited to portfolio optimization, allowing an AI agent to learn the best portfolio mix based on expected returns and risk tolerance.

1. Define the Environment: Stocks in the S&P 500, with daily returns and historical volatility, represent the action space.

2. Reward Function: Set a reward based on portfolio returns adjusted for risk, such as the Sharpe ratio, which considers both return and volatility:

$$\text{Sharpe Ratio} = \frac{\text{Expected Portfolio Return} - \text{Risk-Free Rate}}{\text{Portfolio Volatility}}$$

3. **Q-Value Calculation**: The Q-value represents the expected cumulative reward of selecting a particular action (e.g., buying/selling a stock) given the current state (e.g., market conditions, portfolio balance). The Q-value update rule is:

$$Q(s, a) = Q(s, a) + \alpha \left(r + \gamma \max Q(s', a') - Q(s, a) \right)$$

where:

- s = current state
- a = chosen action
- r = reward from taking action a
- α = learning rate
- γ = discount factor for future rewards

4. Training and Iteration: Over many iterations, the agent learns to select actions that maximize the Sharpe ratio, resulting in an optimized portfolio with favorable risk-return characteristics.

Example Calculation

Suppose the current Q-value for buying a stock is 5, the immediate reward (daily return) is 1, and the maximum future Q-value from the new state is 6. Using a learning rate of 0.1 and a discount factor of 0.9, the updated Q-value would be:

$$Q(\text{buy}) = 5 + 0.1 \left(1 + 0.9 \cdot 6 - 5 \right) = 5 + 0.1 \times 1.4 = 5.14$$

By iterating this process, the RL model converges on an optimal action policy, achieving a balanced portfolio that adjusts dynamically to market conditions.

Real-World Impact

This reinforcement learning approach allows institutional investors to maximize returns while maintaining risk within acceptable bounds. A well-optimized portfolio can generate consistent annual returns with lower volatility than traditional investment strategies, contributing to better risk-adjusted performance.

4. Real-Time Risk Management with Machine Learning

In high-frequency trading (HFT) and other fast-paced financial environments, real-time risk management is critical. Machine learning algorithms can provide instant risk assessments, allowing firms to adjust their positions in response to market conditions.

Example: Managing Market Risk with Gaussian Mixture Models (GMM)

Gaussian Mixture Models (GMMs) are unsupervised learning algorithms that can model complex data distributions, making them useful in identifying clusters within financial data that signify different market regimes (e.g., bull or bear markets).

1. Feature Selection: Gather data on daily returns, volatility, trading volume, and interest rates.

2. Modeling Market Regimes: Using GMM, group the data into clusters representing different market conditions (e.g., high volatility, low volatility). Each cluster is characterized by its mean and covariance, providing a mathematical description of its risk profile.

3. Calculating Risk Exposure: For each trading day, classify the market condition based on GMM clusters and adjust trading positions to minimize exposure to high-risk clusters.

Numerical Example

Suppose the model classifies the current market as a high-volatility regime with a mean return of -0.5% and standard deviation of 2%. A risk-averse strategy might reduce position sizes by 50% during this period to limit potential losses.

This approach enables trading firms to minimize drawdowns and maintain profitability across market cycles. By adjusting risk exposure in real time, firms can protect their assets from sudden market shocks.

5. Fraud Detection Using Anomaly Detection Algorithms

Financial fraud detection is essential to prevent significant losses in online banking, credit card transactions, and other financial activities. AI models, particularly anomaly detection algorithms, can flag unusual transactions for further investigation.

Example: Detecting Anomalies in Credit Card Transactions

1. Data Collection: Analyze transaction data including transaction amount, merchant category, transaction frequency, and geographical location.

2. Applying Anomaly Detection: Use algorithms like Isolation Forest, which works by identifying data points that deviate significantly from the norm. These models can calculate an "anomaly score" for each transaction.

3. Threshold Setting: Transactions with anomaly scores exceeding a set threshold (e.g., 0.8) are flagged as potentially fraudulent.

Example Calculation

Suppose the anomaly score for a transaction is 0.85, and the threshold for flagging is set at 0.8. The transaction would be flagged for review, and a subsequent alert would be sent to the customer for verification.

Real-World Impact

By implementing anomaly detection, financial institutions can reduce false positives, enhance customer satisfaction, and save millions in potential fraud losses. Modern AI-based fraud detection systems are often 80-90% more effective than traditional rule-based systems.

The practical applications of AI in finance go beyond mere predictions, deeply influencing how financial institutions handle forecasting, risk management, portfolio optimization, and fraud detection. From quantitative trading to real-time risk management, AI's ability to process and interpret large datasets allows financial institutions to operate more effectively and profitably. Through examples and calculations, we see the measurable impact of AI across various aspects of finance, offering businesses not only improved performance but also a roadmap to adapt to evolving market conditions dynamically.

CHAPTER 3: COMPETITIVE ADVANTAGE THROUGH STRATEGIC AI IMPLEMENTATION

I n today's fast-paced business landscape, where innovation and technology seem to drive every competitive edge, companies increasingly look to artificial intelligence (AI) and game theory as powerful tools to not only stay relevant but to lead. This chapter explores how the integration of AI and game theory can be a game-changer in gaining a competitive advantage, specifically in understanding and anticipating rivals' moves, improving customer targeting, and streamlining operational efficiency. Together, these approaches redefine traditional business strategy, offering companies a forward-thinking edge that's hard to ignore.

1. The Strategic Intersection of AI and Game Theory

AI and game theory share a common thread: both are designed to predict, optimize, and adapt based on evolving inputs. Game theory, traditionally a framework for understanding competitive and cooperative dynamics, helps businesses model scenarios to assess competitor responses, customer behaviors, and optimal strategies. When layered with AI's predictive and adaptive capabilities, these models become powerful, transforming theoretical assumptions into actionable insights grounded in real-time data.

In a traditional game theory model, a company could estimate a competitor's reaction to a price cut, product launch, or market expansion. However, combining this with AI-driven data analytics means decisions are not just predictions based on historical patterns—they become dynamic, real-time responses capable of recalibrating as new information emerges. AI can mine vast amounts of unstructured data, analyze competitors' past strategies, identify trends, and flag anomalies that suggest shifts in strategy.

Imagine a situation where a leading retailer uses AI to track pricing changes across a competitor's inventory. The system detects a gradual price reduction on select items, signifying a likely strategy shift towards budget-conscious consumers. Through game-theoretic modeling, the retailer can assess various responses, from lowering its own prices to improving its value-add offerings, aiming to outmaneuver its competitor by either matching or countering the rival's moves effectively.

2. The Role of Predictive Modeling in Competitive Strategy

Predictive modeling allows companies to forecast various competitive scenarios, equipping decision-makers with data-driven insights to understand and anticipate the moves of competitors. In the past, these insights might have been limited to historical data trends, leaving blind spots when rivals changed tactics. AI changes this. Advanced machine learning algorithms can recognize patterns in competitors' behaviors faster and more accurately, picking up on subtle clues and warning signs.

For instance, a technology firm could leverage AI-powered predictive modeling to monitor its competitors' research and development spending, patent filings, or hiring practices. Suppose it notices an increase in hiring for machine learning and AI roles within a specific competitor's organization. This might signal an upcoming pivot toward AI-enhanced products, giving the firm a strategic lead time to develop competing products or target segments in advance.

Moreover, by blending these predictive models with game theory, companies can simulate outcomes based on various moves, identifying potential equilibria where their strategies might intersect or diverge from their rivals'. This capability allows businesses to pivot quickly, shifting resources or adjusting tactics when the model signals increased competition or heightened customer interest in alternative solutions.

3. Enhancing Customer Targeting Through AI-Driven Insights

In today's data-rich environment, understanding customers and their shifting needs has become a cornerstone of competitive advantage. AI allows companies to mine customer data far more effectively than traditional methods, helping brands move from general demographic targeting to highly personalized, real-time engagement.

By employing AI in customer targeting, companies can analyze past buying patterns, browsing behaviors, and even social media interactions to build customer profiles that feel almost intuitive. For example, an e-commerce platform could use AI to determine which products a customer is most likely to purchase based on current trends, past purchases, and market sentiment. This real-time intelligence enables the platform to dynamically adjust recommendations, boosting conversion rates and customer satisfaction.

When AI is combined with game theory, customer targeting strategies become even sharper. With game theory, the focus shifts to understanding how competitors might react to the same data insights. For example, if an AI model predicts an emerging interest in a new fitness trend, a sportswear company can develop targeted marketing strategies to capture this audience before competitors catch on. Game theory can then predict how these competitors might respond—perhaps by launching similar products, offering discounts, or increasing marketing in the same segment. With this insight, the sportswear brand can anticipate and counteract competitor moves by building loyalty programs, ramping up promotions, or creating exclusive products to retain customer interest.

4. Operational Efficiency as a Competitive Advantage

Beyond external competition and customer targeting, AI has enormous potential to drive internal efficiency, allowing businesses to optimize operations from supply chain management to resource allocation. Efficiency-driven AI tools can improve everything from inventory control to energy management, resulting in leaner, more responsive organizations.

Consider a manufacturing company implementing AI for predictive maintenance. By constantly monitoring equipment and analyzing performance metrics, the company can predict when a machine is likely to fail, scheduling maintenance proactively. This approach not only reduces downtime but also lowers operational costs. When combined with game theory, this operational efficiency becomes part of a larger competitive strategy. If the company operates in an industry where downtime directly impacts market share, its ability to remain operational while competitors face delays provides a strategic advantage.

Additionally, AI can optimize workforce allocation by analyzing historical data on employee performance, customer demand, and project timelines. Using game theory, companies can model scenarios in which competitor companies face resource constraints, allowing them to strategically expand market reach during key opportunities. This approach enables businesses to operate in a way that's not only more cost-effective but also strategically advantaged.

5. The Future of Competitive AI and Game Theory in Business Strategy

AI and game theory are only growing in their significance, as more companies understand the power of data-driven, adaptive strategies. Future business leaders will need to build teams that combine both technical AI proficiency and a strong grounding in strategic thinking, leveraging game theory as a strategic tool.

Emerging AI trends, such as explainable AI and reinforcement learning, will only add to this capability. Explainable AI, which enables transparency in machine decisions, will help executives understand the "why" behind model recommendations, making it easier to assess risks and act quickly on strategic insights. Reinforcement learning, meanwhile, will allow businesses to simulate endless competitive scenarios, helping them identify winning strategies with minimal risk.

Consider a financial services firm utilizing reinforcement learning to test different pricing structures for its credit products. The model experiments with various rates, observing which lead to the highest returns while minimizing defaults. Through game theory, the firm can anticipate competitor responses to different pricing strategies, ensuring they strike the right balance between profitability and market positioning.

In another example, retailers could use reinforcement learning to optimize inventory based on customer demand predictions, adjusting quickly in response to seasonal trends, economic shifts, or competitor moves. This agility, combined with the predictive power of AI, could mark the difference between a company that merely survives and one that thrives.

6. Ethical Considerations and Challenges

Despite the immense promise, integrating AI and game theory into business strategy also raises ethical concerns. AI, when used responsibly, can create immense value. However, companies must remain mindful of privacy, transparency, and fairness. When AI is used to predict competitors' moves or target customers, it's essential to ensure that data is handled ethically and that insights derived don't overstep regulatory or ethical boundaries.

Furthermore, the complexity of integrating AI with game theory models presents significant challenges, requiring investment in technology, data infrastructure, and skilled personnel. For companies without access to substantial resources, there is a risk of falling behind, creating a competitive landscape where only well-funded organizations can keep pace.

Incorporating AI and game theory into strategic planning offers a transformative path for businesses looking to gain a competitive edge. From accurately forecasting competitor moves to enhancing customer engagement and streamlining internal operations, this combination holds the key to an agile, data-driven future. Companies that embrace AI with a strategic, ethical mindset will be well-positioned to lead their industries, setting new standards for innovation, efficiency, and customer engagement. The future of business is here, and it's driven by AI—powered by data and perfected through the lens of game theory.

Real-World Cases of Strategic AI and Game Theory in Action

Exploring abstract theories is one thing; seeing them applied successfully in real business cases is another. This chapter dives into three specific cases where companies have harnessed the combined power of AI and game theory to gain significant competitive advantages. Through real-world examples, we see how these strategies are used to anticipate competitors' moves, enhance customer targeting, and streamline operations. These cases involve tech giant Amazon, the sportswear leader Nike, and global finance player JPMorgan Chase—each demonstrating unique applications of AI and game theory.

Case Study 1: Amazon – Outmaneuvering Competitors in E-commerce

Amazon is one of the world's most successful companies, with a staggering global market share and a dominant position in e-commerce. Behind this success lies a relentless strategy that uses AI and game theory to keep competitors at bay, optimize customer targeting, and create operational efficiencies that few can rival.

Strategic Use of Predictive Modeling and Game Theory

Amazon's predictive algorithms don't just personalize product recommendations for individual users—they also analyze competitor behaviors in real time. Amazon's AI tracks product pricing, availability, and customer reviews across competitor platforms, using this data to adjust its own offerings. If a competitor begins offering a popular product at a discount, Amazon can swiftly respond by either lowering prices or enhancing value propositions through bundled offers or exclusive deals. This agile response, based on game-theoretic modeling, allows Amazon to stay one step ahead of competitors.

To ensure the accuracy of its predictions, Amazon combines AI with historical data and behavioral insights, allowing it to build simulations of potential competitive scenarios. This means the company can predict how other e-commerce giants, like Walmart or Alibaba, might react to Amazon's moves, enabling Amazon to adjust its strategy proactively. Game theory allows Amazon to evaluate whether aggressive pricing, exclusive deals, or faster delivery options will yield the best competitive advantage.

Enhancing Customer Targeting with AI

Amazon's recommendation engine, powered by machine learning algorithms, uses customers' browsing and purchase history to create personalized recommendations. But Amazon doesn't stop there. The company continually refines its algorithms based on competitor actions and seasonal trends. If a competitor launches a holiday campaign targeting high-value electronics, Amazon's AI algorithms will adapt, suggesting comparable or complementary products to customers who might be swayed by these campaigns.

This predictive personalization extends across Amazon's vast ecosystem, from Prime Video recommendations to suggested Alexa skills, creating a cohesive customer experience that strengthens brand loyalty. With AI-driven targeting refined by game theory, Amazon can keep customers engaged, lowering the likelihood that they'll explore alternatives.

Operational Efficiency as a Strategic Edge

Amazon's approach to operational efficiency is another aspect where AI and game theory converge. The company's use of AI for demand forecasting and inventory management is well-documented, with algorithms predicting which products will see spikes in demand and adjusting inventory accordingly. By combining this with game theory, Amazon can also factor in competitors' likely stocking strategies, allowing Amazon to avoid overstocking or understocking key items.

Amazon's AI-powered warehouse robots and optimization systems, like the "Kiva" robots, streamline order fulfillment processes, reducing costs and processing times. This operational advantage enables Amazon to offer fast delivery, including same-day options in some markets, setting a high bar that is difficult for competitors to match. Through this combination of efficiency and competitive foresight, Amazon solidifies its position as an industry leader.

Case Study 2: Nike – Innovating Customer Experience and Market Positioning

Nike, the sportswear giant, has leveraged AI and game theory to become a powerhouse in customer engagement and market differentiation. As the sportswear industry grows more competitive, Nike has adopted technology to maintain and expand its influence, turning to AI to improve customer experiences and utilizing game theory to strategically navigate competitive dynamics.

Predicting Competitor Moves with Game Theory

Nike faces constant competition from brands like Adidas, Puma, and Under Armour. To stay ahead, Nike uses a combination of AI-driven analytics and game theory to anticipate competitors' product launches, marketing campaigns, and pricing adjustments. For instance, Nike's AI systems monitor social media, athlete endorsements, and industry news for hints of rival companies' strategies. Using game theory, Nike's strategic team can simulate various responses, assessing the potential outcomes of price adjustments, product differentiation, or exclusive partnerships.

In preparation for new product lines, Nike can predict how competitors might respond to its innovations. If a competitor is likely to release a similar product at a lower price point, Nike might focus on premium positioning and enhanced product quality to differentiate its offerings, retaining market share through brand prestige rather than price competition. Game theory allows Nike to continuously refine these strategies based on real-time data, keeping competitors on the defensive.

Enhanced Customer Targeting through Personalized Experiences

Nike has embraced AI to elevate customer targeting, especially through its digital ecosystem of apps like Nike Run Club and SNKRS. These platforms collect data on user preferences, exercise habits, and purchase history, allowing Nike to deliver highly personalized recommendations and exclusive product releases. Using machine learning, Nike's apps can suggest specific workout gear based on a user's recent activities, while the SNKRS app sends push notifications to fans about limited-edition sneakers tailored to their tastes.

Nike's personalization strategy is enhanced by game-theoretic insights. For example, if data reveals that a rival brand is launching a product in a category Nike dominates, Nike can leverage exclusive drops or offer early access to loyal customers, creating a sense of urgency and exclusivity that limits competitors' traction. This approach not only boosts customer loyalty but also positions Nike as a brand that understands and anticipates customer needs.

Operational Efficiency in Manufacturing and Distribution

Nike has integrated AI in its supply chain, particularly in manufacturing and distribution. The company uses predictive algorithms to manage inventory levels, balancing supply with projected demand. Game theory comes into play by modeling competitors' manufacturing timelines and release schedules, allowing Nike to adjust production accordingly. If a competitor is expected to release a new running shoe in high volumes, Nike can strategically limit its own supply of a comparable product to drive exclusivity and demand, ensuring that Nike's products retain their premium market position.

Nike's operational strategy extends to sustainable manufacturing. The company uses AI to optimize material sourcing and reduce waste, while game-theoretic models assess potential competitor responses to Nike's sustainable initiatives. This positions Nike as a leader in sustainability while maintaining cost-effective operations, giving it an edge over competitors that lack similar efficiencies.

Case Study 3: JPMorgan Chase – Reinventing Financial Services with AI and Strategic Foresight

JPMorgan Chase, one of the world's largest financial institutions, has pioneered the use of AI and game theory in the financial sector. In an industry where small margins and regulatory shifts can have significant impacts, JPMorgan uses these tools to gain insights into competitor strategies, enhance customer targeting, and ensure operational resilience.

Predicting Market Movements and Competitor Strategies

The financial sector is inherently competitive, with firms vying for market share and customer trust. JPMorgan uses AI to monitor competitors' offerings, track stock market trends, and analyze economic indicators. By integrating game theory, JPMorgan can model the likely reactions of competitors to its strategic moves, from fee adjustments to new product launches.

For instance, if a competitor introduces a new investment product targeting high-net-worth individuals, JPMorgan's AI system can analyze client preferences and simulate different market responses. Game theory enables JPMorgan to predict whether matching the competitor's offering, differentiating through unique features, or adjusting fees will yield the best outcome. This proactive approach allows JPMorgan to maintain a strong market position and client loyalty, even as competitors push for innovation.

Enhanced Customer Targeting and Risk Management

JPMorgan's AI algorithms analyze customer data to offer personalized investment recommendations, credit approvals, and spending insights. Using machine learning, the bank can create individual financial profiles based on income, spending habits, and financial goals, offering customers a tailored experience that builds trust and engagement. Through game-theoretic modeling, JPMorgan can also anticipate competitors' likely responses to its customer retention strategies, allowing the bank to adjust and refine its approaches in real time.

Risk management, another critical area for JPMorgan, benefits significantly from AI and game theory. The bank's AI models assess market risk by analyzing historical data, industry trends, and real-time market shifts. Game theory is applied to understand how competitors might react to economic downturns or regulatory changes, helping JPMorgan mitigate potential losses and capitalize on opportunities when others may struggle.

Operational Efficiency through Process Automation

AI-driven automation at JPMorgan is transforming back-office functions, from data entry to compliance checks. The bank uses machine learning algorithms to streamline processes, cutting costs and reducing errors. Game theory is applied in areas like trading and risk management, where JPMorgan can simulate competitor responses to different financial maneuvers. For instance, if competitors begin adjusting their portfolios in response to market volatility, JPMorgan can simulate scenarios to determine the best strategy to maximize returns while minimizing risk.

The bank's AI-powered chatbots also offer real-time customer service, enabling faster response times and improving customer satisfaction. This operational efficiency not only strengthens JPMorgan's position in the competitive financial services market but also helps it maintain customer trust and loyalty, even as other banks scramble to implement similar technologies.

From Amazon's e-commerce dominance to Nike's customer-centric innovation and JPMorgan Chase's strategic foresight, these companies exemplify the benefits of combining AI with game theory. Each company's ability to predict competitor actions, enhance customer engagement, and streamline operations is a testament to the transformative power of these technologies. As industries become more dynamic and competitive, businesses that embrace AI and game theory will find themselves not only surviving but thriving, paving the way for a new era of intelligent strategy and sustainable growth.

Company	Application Area	AI & Game Theory Strategy	Key Metrics & Impact
Amazon	Predictive Modeling & Competitor Analysis	Real-time competitor price tracking, adjustments, and bundling strategies	**Increased market share:** 38% in U.S. e-commerce market
	Customer Targeting & Personalization	Personalized recommendations based on user behavior and competitor insights	**Conversion Rate Increase:** 35% through personalized recommendations
	Operational Efficiency	Inventory optimization with AI and warehouse automation (Kiva robots)	**Fulfillment Speed:** Reduced average shipping time by 30%
Nike	Competitor Strategy & Product Positioning	Monitoring rival launches, exclusive drops to preempt competitor moves	**Revenue Increase:** 20% in regions with exclusive launches
	Customer Targeting through Digital Apps	Personalized product recommendations via Nike Run Club and SNKRS apps	**Customer Retention Rate:** 3x higher with app engagement
	Sustainable Operations	AI-driven manufacturing and waste reduction	**Sustainability Impact:** 30% reduction in manufacturing waste

JPMorgan Chase	Market Analysis & Competitor Modeling	AI for analyzing competitor products, financial fee adjustments	**Client Retention:** Improved by 25% in high-net-worth segment
	Customer Targeting & Risk Management	Personalized financial products, dynamic risk assessment	**Risk Reduction:** 40% lower exposure during market volatility
	Operational Efficiency in Compliance	AI automation for back-office tasks and compliance checks	**Cost Savings:** 20% reduction in operational costs

CHAPTER 4: FINANCIAL RISK MANAGEMENT IN THE AI ERA

I n this chapter, we explore how AI and game theory revolutionize financial risk management. You'll learn actionable strategies to anticipate risks, protect assets, and turn market volatility into strategic opportunities. Through case studies and cutting-edge examples, you'll discover how companies proactively address risks in today's digital-first, data-rich environment.

The New Face of Financial Risk

The evolution of financial markets over the past decade has introduced unprecedented volatility and complex risks. From unexpected global events to rapid technological shifts, the factors driving financial instability are increasingly difficult to predict and mitigate. The impact of AI on these dynamics is profound, and when combined with the principles of game theory, it provides a powerful framework for reimagining financial risk management.

AI technologies—ranging from machine learning to natural language processing—enable us to analyze immense volumes of data and make decisions in real-time. Game theory, on the other hand, offers insights into competitive behaviors, helping companies foresee and outmaneuver potential threats. Together, they allow for a proactive approach to managing financial risks, turning potential crises into opportunities.

1. Understanding Financial Risks in the Digital Age

In the AI era, financial risk comes in many forms, including:

- Market Risks: Fluctuations in prices, currency exchange rates, and commodity costs.

- Operational Risks: Risks arising from system failures, cyber-attacks, and human error.

- Credit Risks: The possibility that a borrower will fail to repay their obligations.

- Systemic Risks: Risks that affect the entire financial system, often triggered by major events like economic downturns or pandemics.

AI helps address these risks by identifying early warning signals from data that were previously inaccessible or hard to interpret. For instance, machine learning algorithms can analyze real-time transaction data and spot trends before they impact financial stability. Game theory, by contrast, models potential responses from competitors, partners, or even market segments, enabling firms to anticipate and respond to these risks before they escalate.

2. The Role of Game Theory in Financial Risk Management

Game theory helps businesses understand competitive dynamics. In financial risk management, it's used to simulate potential actions by other market players and predict their responses. For instance, in managing currency risk, companies can use game theory to model how foreign governments, financial institutions, and competitors might react to currency fluctuations.

One popular game theory approach is the "Prisoner's Dilemma" model, which analyzes cooperative vs. competitive strategies. In financial contexts, this model helps identify situations where mutual cooperation could reduce risk but competitive actions might increase market volatility. Firms can thus strategically choose to hedge, diversify, or take calculated risks.

3. Proactive Risk Management with AI

Traditional risk management is largely reactive, relying on historical data to inform strategies. AI, however, allows for proactive risk management. By leveraging predictive analytics and real-time data, companies can foresee potential risks and adapt strategies dynamically.

Example: AI-Powered Market Volatility Forecasting

Machine learning models can analyze historical price patterns, social media sentiment, and economic indicators to predict future volatility. Firms can use this data to adjust asset allocation, hedge against potential losses, or even capitalize on predicted downturns. For instance, Natural Language Processing (NLP) models can analyze news articles, social media feeds, and financial reports to detect early signals of a crisis—long before traditional analysts could have identified them.

Example: Portfolio Management with Reinforcement Learning

Reinforcement learning, an AI technique, allows portfolio managers to continuously improve asset allocation strategies based on market feedback. By simulating different asset allocations, this model learns to maximize returns while minimizing risk exposure, ensuring that portfolios are optimized for both stability and growth.

4. Dynamic Asset Protection Strategies

In the AI era, asset protection is no longer just about minimizing loss—it's about making calculated, agile decisions to protect and grow value.

4.1 Stress Testing with AI

Stress testing is a common method of assessing risk tolerance. However, AI-powered stress testing can simulate far more complex scenarios than traditional models. Companies can, for example, test how their assets would fare under various economic shocks, geopolitical changes, or even natural disasters. AI also enables firms to simulate interdependent risks, providing a clearer picture of cascading impacts.

4.2 Real-Time Risk Adjustments

AI-driven systems monitor asset values in real time, adjusting risk profiles as necessary. For example, if an algorithm detects an impending downturn in a specific sector, it can recommend adjustments to portfolios to minimize exposure to that sector. This real-time adaptability provides firms with a crucial advantage, allowing them to pivot their strategies instantly in response to market shifts.

5. Case Study: AI and Game Theory in Action

Consider the financial strategy of a multinational corporation managing a portfolio of global assets. By integrating AI and game theory, the company developed a system that monitors geopolitical risks, economic indicators, and competitor movements in real time. When the system flagged a potential shift in international tariffs that would impact commodity prices, the company preemptively adjusted its hedging strategies, minimizing potential losses.

Here's how they did it:

1. Data Aggregation: They combined data from financial reports, government publications, and market indices to gauge economic stability across regions.

2. Predictive Modeling: Using AI, they forecasted the likelihood of tariff changes and their potential impact on supply chains.

3. Game Theory Application: The company then simulated responses from other market players—predicting how competitors might adjust prices or alter their sourcing strategies.

4. Proactive Adjustment: With this data, the firm diversified its portfolio and adjusted sourcing strategies, effectively mitigating risks long before tariffs actually changed.

This approach highlights the power of AI and game theory in financial risk management, transforming a potential crisis into a controlled, manageable scenario.

6. Implementing AI and Game Theory in Financial Strategy

For businesses aiming to apply AI and game theory to financial risk management, here are key steps:

6.1 Invest in Data Infrastructure

Successful AI models rely on high-quality data. Companies should ensure they have the systems in place to collect, store, and process large amounts of data in real time. Data sources might include financial transactions, market data, economic indicators, and even social media sentiment.

6.2 Develop Cross-Functional Expertise

Combining AI and game theory requires both technical expertise and business acumen. Data scientists, financial analysts, and strategists must collaborate to interpret data and implement insights effectively.

6.3 Prioritize Ethical and Transparent AI

AI models in financial risk management must be transparent and free from bias, especially as regulatory scrutiny increases. Ethical AI practices not only protect firms legally but also build customer trust.

Financial risk management in the AI era is about more than just surviving volatility—it's about thriving within it. By combining the predictive power of AI with the strategic foresight of game theory, firms can transform their risk management approaches, anticipating challenges and seizing new opportunities. The result is a resilient, agile organization capable of navigating even the most turbulent markets with confidence.

Key Issues Addressed by AI and Game Theory in Financial Risk Management

1. Issue 1: Predicting and Mitigating Market Volatility

Market volatility has always been a significant challenge in finance. Price fluctuations, economic cycles, and unexpected events like global crises can destabilize entire portfolios, leaving companies vulnerable to severe losses. Traditional methods for managing market volatility rely heavily on historical data and trend analysis, which can be insufficient in predicting rapid or unprecedented shifts.

How AI and Game Theory Address Market Volatility

AI enhances traditional approaches by analyzing and integrating data in real time from diverse sources, including global news feeds, social media, and economic indicators. AI can detect subtle patterns and early warning signs that human analysts or conventional models might miss. For example, Natural Language Processing (NLP) scans millions of articles, posts, and reports, helping organizations identify trends that could impact their financial positions.

Game Theory for Strategic Positioning

Game theory enables companies to anticipate and model competitor responses during times of high volatility. If a tech giant decides to change its pricing strategy, game theory can simulate how other competitors might react, allowing a company to adjust its strategy to maintain a competitive edge. This proactive approach means that instead of reacting to market changes, companies can prepare for various scenarios, significantly mitigating their risks.

Example Case: A retail giant uses AI and game theory to forecast seasonal consumer behavior and competitor responses. By analyzing online shopping trends and social sentiment, they can better prepare for sales dips or price wars, staying a step ahead in volatile market conditions.

2. Issue 2: Reducing Credit and Counterparty Risks

Credit risk, or the risk that a borrower will default on their obligations, remains one of the most pressing issues in finance. As companies extend credit or enter into agreements with counterparties, they face the challenge of accurately assessing the risk involved. Traditional credit risk assessments are based on financial ratios and credit scores, which may not reflect sudden changes in a company's ability to repay.

How AI and Game Theory Address Credit and Counterparty Risks

AI-driven predictive models provide a dynamic way to assess creditworthiness by considering real-time economic factors and non-traditional indicators. For instance, AI algorithms can analyze a company's transactions, revenue fluctuations, and even sentiment indicators from employee or customer reviews, providing a holistic view of financial health.

Game theory further enhances this process by modeling the behavior of counterparty risks. For instance, if a supplier faces financial challenges, game theory can help predict how they might act under stress, allowing companies to preemptively adjust their strategies. This predictive power is especially useful in uncertain economic environments, where the risk of default may increase unpredictably.

Credit Risk Evaluation in Action

Example Case: A multinational bank employs AI models to monitor client risk profiles continuously. If the algorithm detects a potential risk factor, such as declining revenue trends or adverse social media sentiment, it can flag the account for review. Game theory helps the bank assess what would happen if they reduce credit exposure to the client, considering how other financial institutions might react.

3. Issue 3: Enhancing Operational Efficiency and Decision-Making

In financial risk management, quick and informed decisions are essential to avoid potential losses. Traditional decision-making models can be too slow or too narrow, especially when dealing with real-time threats such as cyber-attacks, regulatory changes, or supply chain disruptions. Operational inefficiencies, outdated data, and lack of visibility into real-time data compound these risks.

How AI and Game Theory Enhance Operational Efficiency

AI's automation capabilities streamline operations by processing vast amounts of data and providing actionable insights, eliminating human bottlenecks. Automated AI systems can monitor risk indicators continuously and alert relevant teams before an issue escalates.

Game theory enhances decision-making by simulating potential scenarios, allowing organizations to make preemptive choices. For example, companies can run simulations to explore various supplier, partner, or competitor responses in a range of "what-if" situations. These simulations save time and resources and provide confidence in decision-making even under pressure.

Operational Efficiency in Action

Example Case: A logistics company uses AI to optimize routes and inventory, minimizing operational costs. Game theory simulates responses to supply chain disruptions, providing a model for alternative strategies. This way, the company remains agile and prepared for unexpected challenges, ensuring continuous operation with minimal risk.

AI and game theory together transform financial risk management by solving complex problems that traditional models cannot. With predictive analysis, enhanced credit assessment, and streamlined decision-making, these technologies equip companies to thrive in an increasingly volatile financial landscape. This future-proof approach ensures resilience, adaptability, and a strategic edge in handling the financial risks of tomorrow.

CHAPTER 5: CASE STUDIES IN GAME THEORY AND AI: REAL-WORLD APPLICATIONS

The rapid integration of Artificial Intelligence (AI) and Game Theory into business strategy is transforming industries and disrupting traditional models. For businesses, adopting these technologies is no longer just a competitive advantage—it's a necessity to remain relevant. In this chapter, we'll dive into real-world applications, examining companies that have harnessed the power of AI and Game Theory to gain a strategic edge. Through case studies, we'll explore how they used these tools to innovate, overcome challenges, and ultimately create successful, adaptive strategies. Alongside success stories, we'll also look at common pitfalls, highlighting crucial lessons learned to offer a roadmap for other businesses looking to adopt these cutting-edge approaches.

1. Amazon: Price Optimization and Competitive Positioning

Amazon's rise to dominance in e-commerce has been largely driven by an adaptive pricing strategy, where AI algorithms optimize product prices in real-time based on Game Theory principles. Traditionally, businesses set static prices, but Amazon introduced dynamic pricing, which adjusts prices based on demand, competitor pricing, inventory levels, and customer behavior.

The Game Theory Approach:

Amazon's dynamic pricing strategy is a classic example of a game-theoretic approach to pricing. Amazon essentially "plays" against its competitors by using advanced algorithms that predict competitor moves and price shifts, enabling Amazon to adjust its pricing to gain a strategic advantage. This setup resembles the classic "prisoner's dilemma" in Game Theory: while other e-commerce platforms may also adjust prices, Amazon's ability to automate and predict allows it to optimize profits, even in scenarios where competitors would usually be forced to cut prices.

Lessons Learned:

1. Automation Is Essential: By automating pricing decisions, Amazon reduces reaction time, which is essential in a competitive market. Companies that rely on manual price adjustments risk losing their advantage to automated competitors.

2. Continuous Data Input: Amazon's AI-driven pricing strategies are continually updated with data, enabling the system to improve in real-time. Other businesses adopting a similar model should prioritize consistent, clean data inputs to maximize performance.

3. Dynamic Positioning as a Strategy: Unlike traditional strategies, where companies aim for a fixed market position, Amazon continuously redefines its position relative to competitors. This flexible approach is key to staying relevant in fast-changing markets.

Pitfalls to Avoid:

- Pricing Instability: Dynamic pricing can lead to price volatility, which might frustrate customers. Companies should aim for an optimal balance, ensuring price shifts are subtle enough not to alienate loyal customers.

2. Tesla: Autonomous Vehicle Navigation and the Game of Safety

Tesla's autonomous driving technology leverages Game Theory to address one of its biggest challenges: navigating complex, dynamic traffic environments. By combining AI and Game Theory, Tesla's autonomous vehicles can predict the behavior of surrounding vehicles and make real-time driving decisions, enhancing both efficiency and safety.

The Game Theory Approach:

Tesla's AI algorithms apply Game Theory principles to assess the intentions of nearby drivers, identifying when to yield, accelerate, or take defensive maneuvers. This decision-making process resembles the "hawk-dove" model in Game Theory, where each vehicle's decision to cooperate or compete (in this case, yielding or moving forward) affects the overall system's balance. Tesla's approach also accounts for multiple layers of interaction, recognizing that each car is both a player and an observer in the traffic environment.

Lessons Learned:

1. Safety First: AI models trained with a safety-first perspective prevent aggressive maneuvers that could jeopardize passengers. Game Theory here enables Tesla's cars to avoid high-risk interactions with human drivers.

2. Strategic Predictive Analysis: Predicting driver behavior isn't a perfect science, but using Game Theory has allowed Tesla to develop probabilistic models that estimate likely moves from other drivers, a crucial feature for proactive decision-making.

Pitfalls to Avoid:

- Complexity of Human Behavior: Human drivers don't always act rationally. Tesla must constantly refine its algorithms to handle unpredictable scenarios, highlighting the importance of continuous improvement when deploying AI and Game Theory in real-world applications.

3. Netflix: Recommendation Systems and Customer Retention

Netflix uses AI-based recommendation systems to keep users engaged, directly impacting its bottom line by boosting retention and reducing churn. Netflix applies Game Theory to personalize content recommendations, encouraging users to stay on the platform longer and consume more content.

The Game Theory Approach:

Netflix's recommendation system treats content selection as a cooperative game. The algorithm tries to match users with content that optimizes both engagement (beneficial for Netflix) and satisfaction (beneficial for users). Game Theory is particularly effective here as it helps Netflix balance short-term engagement with long-term satisfaction, a delicate equilibrium that keeps users coming back for more.

Lessons Learned:

1. User Behavior Analysis: Understanding user preferences helps Netflix tailor content in a way that feels both organic and highly personal, underscoring the value of user-centric design.

2. Multi-Stage Interaction: Netflix doesn't just consider a single user interaction but examines the entire viewing journey. This multi-stage perspective in Game Theory ensures that Netflix maximizes both user satisfaction and engagement over time.

Pitfalls to Avoid:

- Over-Personalization: Recommendations can become repetitive, which might disengage users. Netflix's AI must avoid the trap of only recommending familiar content, balancing discovery with personalization.

4. Google: Ad Auctions and Revenue Maximization

Google's ad auction system is a prime example of AI and Game Theory in action, where advertisers bid for ad placement on the search results page. Using Game Theory, Google maximizes ad revenue by creating an auction model that incentivizes advertisers to bid their true value.

The Game Theory Approach:

Google's ad auctions operate on a generalized second-price auction system, where the highest bidder doesn't pay their bid but instead pays a penny more than the next-highest bid. This setup, inspired by Game Theory's "Vickrey-Clarke-Groves" mechanism, encourages honest bidding, as advertisers know they won't necessarily have to pay their top bid. This approach benefits both Google and advertisers by maximizing ad efficiency and encouraging genuine competition.

Lessons Learned:

1. Transparency Enhances Trust: Google's ad model is designed to build trust with advertisers, as they can bid without fear of being unfairly charged. This trust has contributed to Google's dominance in digital advertising.

2. Optimization Through AI: AI algorithms ensure that ads are shown to users who are most likely to engage, maximizing ROI for advertisers and ad revenue for Google.

Pitfalls to Avoid:

- Market Saturation Risks: Too many advertisers vying for similar keywords can drive up costs, potentially making ads unaffordable for smaller businesses. Google must constantly monitor and balance its auction to ensure broad access to advertisers.

5. Procter & Gamble: Supply Chain Optimization and Game Theory

Procter & Gamble (P&G) adopted Game Theory and AI to streamline its supply chain, enhancing resilience and responsiveness in a competitive market. By using AI and Game Theory, P&G can predict supplier behavior, anticipate disruptions, and optimize delivery routes.

The Game Theory Approach:

P&G's supply chain operates like a complex game of resource allocation, where each supplier and logistics provider represents a "player" with unique motivations. By modeling the entire supply chain as a network of players, P&G's AI can predict and counteract supply bottlenecks or delays. The company employs cooperative Game Theory models to foster partnerships, ensuring each player in the chain benefits and contributes optimally.

Lessons Learned:

1. Cooperative Strategies Work Best: P&G's cooperative model encourages suppliers to align with the company's goals, fostering a collaborative supply chain network that benefits everyone.

2. Predictive Analytics: Using AI to predict demand fluctuations allows P&G to adjust supply routes and stock levels proactively, ensuring consistent availability of products.

Pitfalls to Avoid:

- Over-Dependence on Predictive Models: Supply chains are influenced by factors that AI might not fully anticipate, such as natural disasters or geopolitical events. P&G must balance AI predictions with contingency planning for unpredicted events.

6. Airbnb: Dynamic Pricing and Game Theory in Hospitality

Airbnb's success can be attributed in part to its dynamic pricing model, which leverages Game Theory to set rental rates based on demand, location, and competitor pricing. Hosts using Airbnb's pricing tool benefit from Game Theory as they're equipped to adjust prices based on local demand patterns.

The Game Theory Approach:

Airbnb applies Game Theory's "matching theory," optimizing price points based on host preferences, guest demand, and competitor prices. It's a dynamic, adaptive model that ensures competitive rates for guests and maximized revenue for hosts. Game Theory's influence is particularly visible during peak times, like holidays, when demand spikes and strategic pricing becomes essential.

Lessons Learned:

1. Market Responsiveness: Airbnb's dynamic pricing enables it to respond to changing market conditions in real-time, ensuring high occupancy rates and optimized earnings.

2. Data-Driven Decision Making: Airbnb's algorithm learns from historical data, allowing it to predict demand and adjust pricing to match market dynamics effectively.

Pitfalls to Avoid:

- Price Sensitivity Among Users: Rapid price changes can alienate price-sensitive customers. Airbnb has to ensure that its dynamic pricing is balanced, preventing prices from fluctuating to the point of frustrating customers.

These case studies reveal that combining AI and Game Theory can drive substantial competitive advantages, provided that companies are mindful of potential risks. Key takeaways for businesses considering these technologies include:

1. Prioritize Data Integrity: AI-driven strategies rely on high-quality data. Companies must invest in data management systems to ensure consistent and accurate data inputs.

2. Balance Automation with Human Oversight: While automation accelerates decision-making, human insight remains essential, particularly in areas where AI might misinterpret complex behavior.

3. Adopt a Multi-Stage Strategy: Success in today's competitive landscape often requires adaptability. Businesses should view AI and Game Theory as continuous, multi-stage processes rather than one-time solutions.

4. Test, Learn, and Iterate: Businesses must be prepared to refine their algorithms continuously. Real-world applications are complex, and iterative improvements are crucial for maintaining relevance.

By adopting these strategies, companies can harness the full potential of AI and Game Theory, driving innovation and staying ahead in today's fast-paced business landscape.

Key Challenges and Threats in the Application of Game Theory and AI in Business

The integration of Game Theory and Artificial Intelligence (AI) in business strategy offers promising advantages but is not without substantial risks and challenges. In this chapter, we will delve into the obstacles companies encounter as they apply these advanced tools, with a focus on real-world threats that could impact growth and competitive positioning. These challenges range from data security and ethical concerns to technical difficulties and economic dependencies that can shape or derail strategic plans. Using industry statistics and examples, we'll provide an in-depth examination of the core obstacles, with insights on how businesses can navigate them for long-term success.

1. Data Privacy and Security Concerns

Data privacy and security represent one of the most pressing challenges for companies leveraging AI and Game Theory in their strategies. In a world where data-driven decisions are key to competitive success, the collection, storage, and analysis of vast amounts of data are necessary. However, this dependency also exposes businesses to significant risks. According to a 2022 study by IBM, the global average cost of a data breach reached $4.35 million, a figure that continues to rise with each year as attacks become more sophisticated.

Challenges:

- High Sensitivity of Data: Companies integrating AI need extensive data on consumers, competitors, and suppliers, much of which is highly sensitive. Game Theory applications in pricing, for example, require real-time competitor data, which can inadvertently lead to data privacy violations if not carefully managed.

- Regulatory Constraints: Legislation like the General Data Protection Regulation (GDPR) in the EU imposes strict limitations on data usage. For businesses operating globally, navigating different regulatory environments adds a layer of complexity. Failure to comply can result in fines, as seen with Meta's $1.3 billion GDPR fine in 2023 for unauthorized data transfer.

- Threat of Cyberattacks: As companies accumulate more data, they become prime targets for cybercriminals. For instance, AI-driven pricing models are susceptible to data breaches that could expose sensitive pricing strategies to competitors.

Solutions:

- Invest in Advanced Encryption: Companies must use advanced encryption techniques and secure cloud storage solutions to protect their data.

- Transparent Data Collection Practices: By making data collection practices transparent and obtaining clear user consent, businesses can reduce the risk of regulatory fines and build customer trust.

2. Algorithmic Bias and Ethical Dilemmas

One of the less-discussed but critical risks associated with AI and Game Theory is the potential for algorithmic bias, where AI models make decisions that reflect pre-existing biases in training data. A study by Harvard Business Review found that nearly 60% of AI algorithms showed some form of inherent bias, leading to ethical and reputational issues.

Challenges:

- Bias in AI Training Data: AI algorithms trained on biased data tend to reinforce those biases in real-world applications. For instance, in hiring algorithms, certain demographic groups may be unfairly disadvantaged if historical data reflects systemic biases.

- Unintended Ethical Consequences: Game Theory models are designed to maximize outcomes, which could lead to ethically questionable practices. For example, some dynamic pricing models may charge higher prices in low-income areas if data suggests willingness to pay is lower elsewhere.

- Consumer Backlash: Consumers are increasingly aware of and sensitive to algorithmic bias. Reputational risks can severely impact brand loyalty, as seen in the backlash faced by Apple in 2019 when its credit card algorithm was accused of gender bias.

Solutions:

- Bias Audits: Regular audits of AI algorithms can identify and correct bias, helping companies avoid ethical pitfalls.

- Diverse Data Sources: By using diverse and representative datasets, businesses can help minimize bias in AI models.

3. Complexity of Real-World Implementation

While the theoretical applications of Game Theory and AI offer exciting possibilities, real-world implementation is highly complex. A report by McKinsey reveals that over 70% of companies struggle to scale AI projects, primarily due to operational hurdles and a lack of integration with existing systems.

Challenges:

- Technical Complexity: Game Theory models require sophisticated algorithms that can be difficult to implement and maintain. Furthermore, combining AI with Game Theory to model real-world scenarios necessitates computational power that may not be accessible to all companies.

- High Development Costs: Implementing AI and Game Theory solutions involves substantial upfront investment. According to Deloitte, the average cost for a large-scale AI project in 2023 was around $500,000, not including ongoing maintenance expenses.

- Skills Gap: There is a shortage of professionals with expertise in both Game Theory and AI, making it difficult for companies to find the talent needed to implement these systems effectively.

Solutions:

- Invest in Training Programs: Companies can bridge the skills gap by investing in training programs to develop in-house expertise.

- Modular Implementation: By breaking down complex systems into modular components, companies can incrementally implement Game Theory and AI solutions, reducing initial costs and complexity.

4. Dynamic Pricing and Customer Trust

Dynamic pricing models, which adjust prices based on demand, competition, and other factors, are widely used in e-commerce, hospitality, and transportation. However, the perceived unfairness of fluctuating prices can erode customer trust. According to a survey by Accenture, 52% of consumers feel that dynamic pricing lacks transparency, creating a risk of alienating loyal customers.

Challenges:

- Perceived Unfairness: Customers often react negatively to sudden price hikes, especially if they feel that the pricing model is exploiting demand.

- Customer Loyalty Risks: Dynamic pricing can harm customer loyalty if consumers feel they are not being treated fairly. For instance, airline companies faced significant criticism during the pandemic for price spikes in flight tickets.

- Complexity in Balancing Demand and Supply: Dynamic pricing models depend on accurate demand forecasts, but sudden changes in customer behavior can lead to inefficiencies and customer dissatisfaction.

Solutions:

- Transparent Pricing Policies: Businesses can mitigate customer concerns by being transparent about how dynamic pricing works and why prices change.

- Loyalty Discounts: Offering loyalty-based discounts or protections can reassure customers and enhance trust.

5. Competition and Imitation Risks

As more businesses adopt AI and Game Theory, competition becomes fiercer, and the risk of imitation grows. According to Gartner, by 2025, 60% of companies will have adopted some form of AI, intensifying competition. Early adopters must therefore constantly innovate to maintain their competitive advantage.

Challenges:

- Competitive Imitation: Competitors can reverse-engineer successful AI models, replicating them to achieve similar results. This imitation dilutes the value of the original investment.

- Falling Margins Due to Saturation: Widespread adoption of AI and Game Theory in pricing strategies can lead to a race to the bottom, especially in industries like e-commerce where competitors constantly undercut each other.

- Patents and Intellectual Property: Protecting proprietary algorithms and models is challenging, and enforcing patents in AI-driven applications remains a gray area.

Solutions:

- Continuous Innovation: To stay ahead, companies must prioritize R&D to evolve their algorithms and maintain a strategic edge.

- IP Protection Strategies: Companies should explore options for intellectual property protection, including trade secrets and patents where applicable.

6. Environmental and Energy Consumption Concerns

AI and Game Theory applications require substantial computational resources. According to OpenAI, training large AI models can consume as much as 284 metric tons of carbon, the equivalent of flying 300 passengers from New York to San Francisco and back. This raises environmental concerns as companies increasingly adopt AI-driven solutions.

Challenges:

- High Energy Consumption: Complex algorithms require intensive computing power, leading to significant energy consumption. This not only raises operational costs but also increases the carbon footprint of businesses.

- Sustainability Reputational Risks: Consumers and stakeholders are increasingly concerned about corporate environmental responsibility. Companies that heavily rely on energy-intensive AI may face backlash or pressure to adopt more sustainable practices.

Solutions:

- Energy-Efficient AI Models: Companies can use optimized algorithms and green cloud solutions that reduce energy consumption.

- Investment in Renewable Energy: Partnering with green energy providers or using renewable energy for data centers can help offset the environmental impact.

7. Regulatory and Legal Uncertainty

As AI applications proliferate, governments worldwide are introducing new regulations to ensure transparency and fairness. However, these regulations vary widely by region, creating compliance challenges for companies operating globally. According to a 2023 PwC report, 65% of CEOs expressed concern over AI regulations, fearing fines, operational restrictions, and reputational damage.

Challenges:

- Changing Regulations: New and evolving regulations in the EU, US, and other regions require companies to frequently update their practices, which can be costly and complex.

- Legal Liability for AI Decisions: Legal frameworks around AI are still under development, and questions about liability for AI-driven decisions remain unresolved. This is particularly relevant in sectors like autonomous driving, where mistakes can lead to accidents and substantial liabilities.

- Antitrust Issues: The use of AI in dynamic pricing and competitive strategy has raised concerns over monopolistic practices, with regulators scrutinizing companies that use algorithms to manipulate markets.

Solutions:

- Compliance as a Core Strategy: Companies should treat regulatory compliance as a core component of their AI strategy, ensuring they have dedicated resources to monitor and implement necessary changes.

- Legal Safeguards: By building legal safeguards into AI models, companies can mitigate risks associated with liability for AI-driven actions.

8. Limitations in Predictive Accuracy Despite advances in AI, predictive models are inherently limited in their accuracy. Game Theory-based models, while powerful, can struggle to account for irrational human behavior and unexpected market fluctuations. While Game Theory provides a robust framework for modeling competitive interactions and strategic decisions, it assumes that players are rational and possess complete or significant information about the game and each other's strategies. In real-world markets, however, irrationality, incomplete information, and unpredictable shifts introduce elements that are difficult to quantify or anticipate accurately.

For instance, human emotions—such as fear during a financial crisis or overconfidence during a booming market—often drive decisions that deviate from the rational strategies Game Theory expects. Similarly, external shocks, like geopolitical conflicts or natural disasters, can abruptly change the "rules of the game" in ways that no model can foresee.

These limitations can cause models to misjudge market movements or underestimate the impact of sudden, high-impact events, also known as "black swans."

The complexity of modern markets, with their high degree of interdependence and rapid information flow, adds another layer of unpredictability. Even with advanced machine learning techniques, models based on historical data may not be able to keep pace with new variables and evolving dynamics. This is particularly evident in fast-changing industries like technology and finance, where innovation and regulation create new norms faster than models can adjust.

As a result, while Game Theory and AI-enhanced predictive models provide valuable insights and strategic guidance, they should be used with caution and continuously updated to incorporate the latest data and real-world developments. Decision-makers must also complement predictive models with qualitative insights and expert judgment to adapt to unexpected shifts, ensuring a more resilient approach to navigating uncertainty.

Game Theory, AI, and Financial Strategy: Redefining the Future of Business

In a world increasingly dominated by data, artificial intelligence (AI), and ever-evolving financial landscapes, business leaders are racing to stay ahead. Game theory, the study of strategic decision-making, has traditionally been a powerful tool in economics, finance, and business. But the intersection of game theory with AI is opening new dimensions for strategic planning, enabling companies to create competitive advantages that were previously unimaginable. This book dives deep into the mechanics of how game theory and AI can redefine business strategies, exploring how these technologies can empower leaders to make smarter decisions, predict competitor behavior, and thrive in volatile markets.

From anticipating competitors' moves to personalizing customer experiences, the integration of game theory and AI is reshaping financial strategy. Businesses are no longer solely dependent on static models; they are dynamically adjusting strategies in real-time, with algorithms analyzing millions of possibilities to offer the optimal course of action. This capability is especially transformative in finance, where risk management and strategic investment decisions hinge on the most accurate information and the swiftest analysis.

Key Takeaways from This Book

1. Revolutionizing Decision-Making: Explore how AI can transform the speed and accuracy of strategic decisions.

2. Enhancing Financial Strategy through Prediction: AI's predictive models allow for far-reaching risk analysis, helping businesses not just react but proactively shape market trends.

3. Implementing Game Theory in Business Contexts: See real-world applications of game theory in negotiations, pricing, and market entry.

4. Ethical Considerations and Limitations: Understand the boundaries of AI and game theory, especially regarding privacy, ethics, and AI's role in decision-making.

This book provides insights on the methods, case studies, and actionable steps to leverage AI and game theory, creating a roadmap to redefine your financial and business strategies in today's competitive environment.

APPENDICES

A Appendix A provides a glossary of essential terms and concepts used throughout the book, offering readers a quick reference to technical language and definitions. These terms cover foundational and advanced ideas in game theory and AI, giving readers a strong conceptual basis to understand the strategic applications discussed in this book.

Key Concepts:

1. Artificial Intelligence (AI): Refers to the simulation of human intelligence in machines designed to perform tasks that typically require human intelligence, such as learning, problem-solving, and decision-making.

2. Game Theory: A mathematical study of strategy and decision-making, particularly in competitive situations where the outcome depends on the actions of multiple players.

3. Machine Learning (ML): A subset of AI that allows systems to learn from data and improve over time without being explicitly programmed. It's essential for building predictive models in business strategy.

4. Nash Equilibrium: A situation in which no player can benefit by changing their strategy while the other players keep theirs unchanged. It's a crucial concept in game theory for analyzing stable outcomes.

5. Payoff Matrix: A tool used in game theory to display the potential outcomes for different decisions. It visually represents the gains or losses for each player based on their choices.

6. Algorithmic Trading: The use of AI algorithms to make rapid trading decisions in financial markets, often leveraging game theory to anticipate market moves and execute profitable trades.

7. Deep Learning: A specialized area of machine learning involving neural networks with multiple layers. It's often used in complex decision-making applications in business and finance.

8. Prisoner's Dilemma: A classic example in game theory illustrating the conflict between individual and collective interest. It's used to explain various strategic decision-making scenarios in business.

9. Pareto Efficiency: A state where resources are allocated optimally, and no one can be made better off without making someone else worse off. This concept helps in understanding efficiency in strategic decisions.

10. Predictive Analytics: The use of data, statistical algorithms, and machine learning to identify future outcomes based on historical data. It's widely used in financial strategy for forecasting market trends.

11. Zero-Sum Game: A situation in game theory where one participant's gain is exactly balanced by the losses of others, a concept crucial in competitive business environments.

12. Decision Trees: A tool used in AI for mapping out possible decisions and their outcomes, benefits, and potential risks, aiding in choosing optimal strategies.

By familiarizing yourself with these concepts, you'll be better prepared to navigate the content of this book and leverage game theory and AI effectively in business strategy.

Appendix B: Practical Tools and Resources for Implementing AI in Strategy

For business leaders and strategists ready to implement AI and game theory concepts in their organizations, this appendix provides a curated list of resources, software, and tools to get started. From basic analytical tools to advanced AI-driven platforms, these resources are designed to facilitate strategic planning, enhance decision-making, and streamline financial analysis.

Recommended Tools and Software:

1. TensorFlow (Google): An open-source platform for machine learning that enables businesses to develop complex models for predictive analytics, useful for everything from customer behavior predictions to risk assessments in finance.

2. IBM Watson: IBM's AI platform offers various tools for data analysis, machine learning, and NLP (natural language processing), ideal for businesses aiming to leverage AI across different departments.

3. MATLAB: A high-performance language for technical computing, widely used for algorithm development, data visualization, and game theory modeling.

4. R Programming Language: A powerful language for statistical computing, especially useful for financial analysts and strategists in creating predictive models and conducting complex data analysis.

5. Microsoft Azure Machine Learning: Azure's cloud-based AI and ML services enable businesses to build, train, and deploy machine learning models at scale, making it accessible for businesses of all sizes.

6. Simulink (MathWorks): A platform for multi-domain simulation and model-based design, beneficial for creating and testing complex financial models using game theory and AI.

7. The Financial Game Theory Toolkit (FGTT): A comprehensive suite of game theory modeling tools designed for financial strategists. It includes payoff matrix tools, equilibrium solvers, and market simulation capabilities.

8. RapidMiner: A data science platform that offers various tools for data preparation, machine learning, and model deployment, useful for both business analytics and strategic planning.

9. KNIME: An open-source software platform for data analytics, reporting, and integration, often used for implementing machine learning and game theory in business settings.

10. PyTorch (Meta): An open-source machine learning library based on the Torch library, PyTorch is popular among researchers and businesses for developing and deploying ML models quickly and effectively.

Books and Guides:

- Machine Learning Yearning by Andrew Ng – A guide to structuring AI projects effectively.

- Artificial Intelligence: A Guide for Thinking Humans by Melanie Mitchell – A comprehensive introduction to AI.

- The Art of Strategy by Avinash K. Dixit and Barry J. Nalebuff – A guide to strategic thinking and game theory for practical business applications.

With these resources, companies can begin integrating AI into their strategic models, using game theory to enhance decision-making frameworks that anticipate competitors' moves and optimize resource allocation.

Appendix C: Additional Readings and Academic Resources

For readers who wish to explore the intricacies of game theory, AI, and financial strategy, Appendix C offers a collection of recommended readings, research articles, and academic resources. These materials are intended for further study and to provide a deeper understanding of the theoretical and practical aspects of these fields.

Recommended Books and Articles:

1. Game Theory for Applied Economists by Robert Gibbons: This book is an essential resource for understanding how game theory applies to real-world economic and business situations.

2. Artificial Intelligence: A Modern Approach by Stuart Russell and Peter Norvig: A comprehensive textbook covering the fundamentals of AI, suitable for both beginners and advanced learners.

3. Predictive Analytics: The Power to Predict Who Will Click, Buy, Lie, or Die by Eric Siegel: A practical guide to understanding the power of predictive analytics in business.

4. Research Articles:

   - "Nash Equilibrium in Strategic Games" – A foundational article on Nash equilibrium, essential for understanding equilibrium concepts in business.

   - "Machine Learning in Asset Management – Part 1: Portfolio Construction" by Marcos López de Prado – This paper discusses the application of machine learning in portfolio management, offering valuable insights for financial strategists.

   - "The Ethics of Artificial Intelligence" – A collection of essays on the ethical considerations surrounding AI, relevant for strategists who need to balance innovation with responsibility.

5. Academic Journals:

   - Journal of Financial Economics: Contains research on topics such as game theory, AI applications in finance, and investment strategy.

   - Journal of Business Research: Covers a wide array of topics in strategic planning, including articles on AI's role in decision-making and competitive strategy.

6. Online Courses and Lectures:

   - Coursera – Game Theory by Stanford University: A comprehensive online course covering game theory fundamentals, including applications in economics and business strategy.

   - edX – Artificial Intelligence by Columbia University: This course provides an in-depth introduction to AI, its applications, and its implications for businesses.

   - MIT OpenCourseWare – Machine Learning with Python: A free course for learning how to apply Python in machine learning, suitable for business professionals looking to implement AI-driven strategies.

These additional readings and resources provide a foundation for those aiming to delve deeper into the fields of AI, game theory, and financial strategy. They offer practical insights and scholarly knowledge, equipping readers with the tools to stay ahead in a rapidly evolving business landscape.

END

www.ingramcontent.com/pod-product-compliance
Lightning Source LLC
Chambersburg PA
CBHW070127230526
45472CB00004B/1462